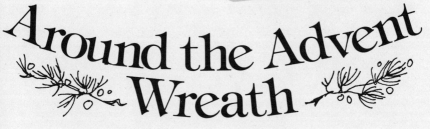

Around the Advent Wreath

DEVOTIONS FOR FAMILIES USING THE ADVENT WREATH

by Nancy Lee Sasser

AUGSBURG PUBLISHING HOUSE

Minneapolis

AROUND THE ADVENT WREATH
Devotions for Families Using the Advent Wreath

Cover art and illustrations by Betty Sievert.

International Standard Book No. 0-8066-2074-9

Copyright © 1984 Augsburg Publishing House

Scripture quotations unless otherwise noted are from the Revised Standard Version of the Bible, copyright 1946, 1952, and 1971 by the Division of Christian Education of the National Council of Churches, and are used by permission.

Scripture quotations from the *Good News Bible (Today's English Version)*, copyright 1966, 1971, and 1976 by American Bible Society, are used by permission.

MANUFACTURED IN THE UNITED STATES OF AMERICA

Using the Advent Wreath

Whether it is a new experience or a family tradition, the use of the Advent wreath in the home is an opportunity. With the wreath Christian families can emphasize that Christmas is about Christ. Rather than making December chiefly a secular, party-filled, gift-giving month, the family shares Christ-centered activities at home as well as in church services and Sunday school programs.

The daily thoughts, prayers, songs, and scripture readings around the wreath draw the family together in shared anticipation of their coming king and Savior, Jesus Christ. The wreath time becomes a spirit-renewing refuge from the demands of the world, and families should jealously guard the time appointed for these daily devotions.

You may want to establish a routine designating who will light and snuff the candles, who will read the scripture passage, who will offer the prayer, and who will lead the singing. That routine should include a set time for Advent wreath devotions. Any time that is convenient to all family members is appropriate, from breakfast to supper to bedtime. The candles in the wreath may be white (an increasingly common choice); blue, symbolizing hope; violet, symbolizing repentance; or red. If violet is used, the third candle should be rose-colored to emphasize the theme of joy.

Advent begins four Sundays before Christmas Day. During the first week only one candle is lit each day, the second week two candles, and so on. Each candle traditionally represents a different theme. In this booklet the themes are **family relationship, peace, joy,** and **love.**

The wreath may be assembled and the introductory story ("Preparing the Advent Wreath," page 4) read the day before Advent begins. Readings continue daily until the day before Christmas Eve. Then use the Christmas Eve devotion.

Preparing the Advent Wreath

This story may be read together in preparation for the first day's Advent wreath activities. This could be Saturday evening before the first Sunday in Advent, or earlier in the day on Sunday.

If children are older and have an adequate attention span, the activity can be combined with the first day's candle-lighting session and lesson.

READ: "Mom, when are we going to put up our Christmas decorations?" Penny asked, bounding into the living room. She had just returned from an outing to the big shopping center with her friend Beth.

"Evergreen Mall has been decorated for weeks already," she continued, panting for breath. "They've got big plastic candy canes and silver snowflakes in every store. There's Santa's workshop, with a real little train you can ride through a tunnel to see the elves working."

"That does sound exciting," Mother nodded. "But do you remember our decorations? Do any of them look like that?"

Penny looked thoughtful. "Well, no," she said. "We always have the nativity scene on the hall table and the candle Grandma made from melted crayons and that big red flower Aunt Joan sends. Oh, and of course the tree. But it's all the same. They're all Christmas decorations, aren't they?"

"Not really," Mother answered. "The Santa and toy shop you saw are things used by stores and even by some families because to them the Christmas season is a jolly, magical time.

"But Christmas is Jesus' birthday. Because our family belongs to Jesus, we want to show our love for him by being very careful about the kinds of decorations we use in our home.

4

"We haven't put up our decorations early, like the stores, because up until now we've been celebrating another season in the church year called Pentecost. But this Sunday is the first day in Advent. Advent is a special time before Christmas when Christians get ready for the arrival of Jesus."

"You mean we can put up our decorations today?" Penny clapped her hands.

Mother laughed. "Not yet. But we are going to start something special today. We're going to set up an Advent wreath."

Penny's brother Chad came in. "I know about that," he said. "You light a new candle each week until Christmas. Jacob's family has one every year."

"Right," said Mom. "We'll do it every day. But we won't just light the candles. We'll have a little story and a prayer to remind us that Christmas is really the birth of our Savior."

"I do forget that sometimes; we're so busy making reindeer and singing about snowmen in school," Penny admitted.

Chad nodded, then added, "And thinking about presents."

"Let's just say that the Advent wreath is a gift from Dad and me to our family this year," Mother said. "Ask Dad to bring in the box from the car trunk. Then we'll set up the the wreath together."

Set up the wreath at this time. Decide who will light the candles on which days and when the family will meet for devotions. Close with prayer.

PRAY: Dear God, let this Advent wreath and the lessons we learn around it help us to love Jesus more every day. Amen

The Candle of

Family Relationship

This week we will explore God's love for us as demonstrated by his gift of relationship — both our earthly families and the privilege of membership in God's family through the birth and death of our Advent King, the baby Jesus.

Sunday   **FIRST WEEK OF ADVENT**

READ: We call this first candle the **family relationship candle.**

As we light this first candle, let's think about our family. God made our family so that we can love and take care of each other.

Light candle.

There are different kinds of families—some with many children, some with one or two children, and some with no children at all. Some families don't have both a mother and father. Some families have grandparents living with them. Let's list all the people in our family. How do we love and take care of each other? *(Discuss.)*

God prepared our family for us with loving care. He prepared a family for the baby Jesus, too. Hundreds of years before Jesus was born, God chose a faithful man he called Abraham. God told Abraham that someday there would be as many people in his family as there are stars in the sky! He told Abraham that kings would belong to his family. We call Abraham's family the Israelites.

Long after Abraham died, God chose a special Israelite family to have a baby boy named Jesus. Just think how excited Abraham would have been if he had known God chose two people from his family — Mary and Joseph — to be the parents of the greatest king of all—King Jesus!

By you all the families of the earth shall bless themselves (Gen. 12:3).

SING: *"Children of the Heavenly Father," first stanza (page 38).*

PRAY: Heavenly Father, families get excited when a baby is born. The whole world gets excited if the baby is a king. We are excited because Jesus, our King, is coming. Thank you for his special family, and thank you for our family, too. Amen

Family waits quietly until candle is snuffed.

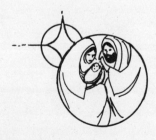

READ: Do you know what ancestors are? They are the relatives who lived a long time before we were born. Abraham was an ancestor of Jesus.

Sara Schmidt's father was in the Air Force. Sara had lived all over the world, but she didn't have a hometown. But Sara knew that her grandparents came from a little village in Germany, where Schmidts had lived for hundreds of years. If she ever went there, she would be welcome. Sara belonged to the village of her ancestors.

As we light this family relationship candle, we think of the many ancestors God placed in the family he prepared for us. Let us think of Jesus' ancestors, too. *(Light candle.)*

One of Jesus' ancestors was an important Israelite king named David. David was born in Bethlehem, so people called Bethlehem the "city of David."

God planned that Jesus would be born in Bethlehem also. This wasn't easy to do, because Jesus' parents lived a long distance from Bethlehem, but God arranged it.

But you, O Bethlehem Ephrathah . . . from you shall come forth for me one who is to be ruler in Israel, whose origin is from old, from ancient days (Micah 5:2).

PRAY: Heavenly Father, thank you for keeping your promise that Jesus would be born in Bethlehem. Amen

SING: O little town of Bethlehem,
How still we see thee lie!
Above thy deep and dreamless sleep
The silent stars go by;
Yet in thy dark streets shineth
The everlasting light.
The hopes and fears of all the years
Are met in thee tonight.

READ: When parents are expecting a child, they want to tell friends and relatives that a baby is on the way. Let's light a candle and see what God told people about his expected Son, Jesus, long before he was born. *(Light candle.)*

For to us a child is born, to us a son is given: and the government will be upon his shoulder, and his name will be called "Wonderful Counselor, Mighty God, Everlasting Father, Prince of Peace" (Isa. 9:6).

Justin's father practiced basketball with him every day. He had been a good player in high school, and he hoped that Justin would like the game, too.

Even when Allison was a little girl she was allowed to plant seeds and arrange flowers in the greenhouse. Her parents hoped she might want to take over the business someday.

Parents have hopes for their children. They hope they will grow up to be happy and fulfilled. Giving parents hopes and dreams, even before a baby is born, is one way God helps parents love and care for their children.

God had a plan for his own Son, Jesus. He knew what Jesus would be when he grew up — he would be the promised Savior. He would be the one who would die on the cross to take away our sins so that we too can be God's sons and daughters.

Today Jesus is known all over the world as the "Prince of Peace."

PRAY: Thank you, Jesus, for taking away my sin. Thank you for doing what your Father hoped and planned. Amen

SING: *"Hark! The Herald Angels Sing," first stanza (page 39).*

READ: . . . Joseph the husband of Mary, of whom Jesus was born, who is called Christ (Matt. 1:16).

"Dad, who is Kevin's father?" Curt asked. "Kevin's last name is McCann, but his dad is Mr. Phillips. Why don't they have the same last name like we do?"

Dad answered, "Kevin's natural father, Mr. McCann, died a few years ago. His mother married Mr. Phillips. Mr. Phillips is a good father to Kevin. He loves and takes care of him and spends time with him. Look at all the model rockets they've made together. But Kevin still goes by his first father's name. So they're both his father, in a way."

As we light this family relationship candle today, we think about fathers. *(Light candle.)* We especially remember the baby Jesus and his father, Joseph. Joseph was Jesus' earthly father. He was a good father. He obeyed all God's commands so that Mary's baby would be born in Bethlehem and grow up safely in Nazareth.

Joseph loved Jesus and fed and clothed him. He taught Jesus to be a carpenter like he was. But Jesus' natural father was someone else. His father was God. When Jesus was baptized, God told many listeners, "This is my beloved Son, with whom I am well pleased."

We are thankful that God chose Joseph to take good care of Jesus so that he could grow up to be the Savior.

SING: *"Children of the Heavenly Father," first and second stanzas (page 38).*

PRAY: Dear God, we love our Dad, and we love you, our heavenly Father. Help us to show this love. Amen

READ: Yesterday as we lit the candle of family relationship we talked about fathers. Can you guess what part of the family we're going to think about today? Yes, mothers. But first here's a story about something that happened at another church. *(Light candle.)*

Every year for the Christmas pageant a fourth-grade girl was chosen to be Mary, the mother of Jesus. Susan couldn't wait to be in the fourth grade because she wanted to be Mary. But when the teacher announced the parts, it wasn't Susan, but Amanda, who was chosen.

Susan didn't think it was fair. Amanda hardly ever came to Sunday school. Susan's teacher could tell she was very disappointed, so she called her aside and explained, "Susan, I know you wanted to be Mary. It is a very special part. But Amanda doesn't get to hear about God's love very often. If she has a chance to be Jesus' mother in our play, perhaps she'll never forget how special Jesus is, even though her parents don't always make sure she comes to church."

Susan nodded. She wanted Amanda to know the Christmas story and to love Jesus as much as she did.

And the angel said to her, "Do not be afraid, Mary, for you have found favor with God" (Luke 1:30).

Probably lots of women would have liked to have been the mother of Jesus. But God chose Mary. She had great faith in God. He knew Mary would be sad when she had to see Jesus die on the cross, but still he chose her, for he knew she would be the right mother for Jesus.

PRAY: Dear God, thank you for choosing the best mother for each of us. Thank you for choosing Mary to be the mother of Jesus. Amen

SING: *"Silent Night," first stanza (page 38).*

READ: "I want the prize," said Carina, opening the cereal box.

"No, I want it. It's my turn!" said Jared.

"I want it!" insisted Carina. "I wish Jesus was my brother. He'd never argue with me!"

Today we'll think about another part of families: brothers and sisters. (*Light candle.*)

Did you know that Jesus had brothers and sisters? Listen to this Bible verse:

Is this not the carpenter, the son of Mary and brother of James and Joses and Judas and Simon, and are not his sisters here with us? (Mark 6:3)

It would be wonderful to have Jesus for a brother. But it might be hard, too. Can you imagine having a brother or sister who never did anything wrong? Jesus never sinned. He was God's perfect Son. But his brothers and sisters were sometimes naughty, just like any boy or girl.

Jesus' brothers loved him, but sometimes they may have been jealous. They didn't even believe he was God's chosen Savior until after he died and rose again.

Sometimes children don't really appreciate brothers and sisters until they're all grown up. But we can try.

Right now, take a turn to say something you like about each brother and sister you have.

SING: "*Children of the Heavenly Father,*" *first and third stanzas (page 38).*

PRAY: Dear heavenly Father, thank you for all our family, and especially for brothers and sisters. We pray for everyone who doesn't know that Christ, our Savior, is born. Amen

READ: This is our last day to light only the family relationship candle. *(Light candle.)*

We feel happy and secure knowing that we all belong together in this family God has prepared for us. We can have an even greater joy knowing we belong to God's family in Jesus. Listen to what Jesus said:

Whoever does the will of God is my brother, and sister, and mother (Mark 3:35).

This is the work of God, that you believe in him whom he has sent (John 6:29).

We have been separated from God. Our sin separates us. God is holy. He can't have sin anywhere near him. But God wants to restore us. He wants to call us back to him.

If we trust the sinless Jesus to take our sin upon himself, then God can let us live with him forever in heaven. We can be in God's family right now. And all because of a little baby born in a manger in Bethlehem almost two thousand years ago!

PRAY: Dear heavenly Father, you did a wonderful thing by having a Son named Jesus. Thank you that we can be called your sons and daughters because of this manner of love. Amen

SING: *"Children of the Heavenly Father," first, second, and third stanzas (page 38).*

The Candle of

Peace

As we light the second candle this week, we focus on the theme of peace. Peace is promised by God both for the individual and for the world through his gift, the baby Jesus, the Prince of Peace.

Sunday　　　　　　　　**SECOND WEEK OF ADVENT**

READ: This week we get to light the second candle as well as the first. We'll call it the **candle of peace.**

Light candles.

The war was over. Now the leaders of two great nations would meet, and the peace treaty would be signed. But first, many arrangements had to be made. A city had to be chosen for the meeting. Schedules and programs had to be worked out in detail.

The leaders sent their helpers ahead of them to prepare everything for the signing of the peace treaty. Only when all was ready did the leaders come.

Because God wanted everyone to be ready for Jesus, he too sent a helper to prepare the people for the arrival of the Prince of Peace. Listen to what the Bible says about this helper:

He will go ahead of the Lord, strong and mighty like the prophet Elijah. He will bring fathers and children together again; he will turn disobedient people back to the way of thinking of the righteous; he will get the Lord's people ready for him (Luke 1:17 TEV).

Can you guess who this helper who came before Jesus was? He was called John the Baptist. John dressed differently than most people and ate strange food, so some people didn't realize he was a peacemaker. But anyone who prepares our hearts to receive Jesus helps bring peace to the world, for from Jesus comes all real peace.

PRAY: Dear God, thank you for John the Baptist, who helped the people get ready for Jesus. Prepare my own heart to welcome my coming Savior. Amen

SING: *"Oh, Come, Oh, Come, Emmanuel," first stanza (page 40).*

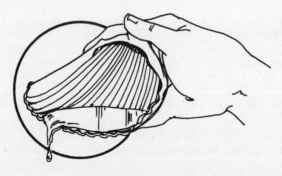

Light candles.

READ: Molly climbed up to the kitchen table where Mom and Dad were busy with cards, envelopes, and stamps.

"Why do our Christmas cards have a dove on them?" she asked, pointing to cards showing a smooth white dove against a dark blue background.

"We want our Christmas card to tell about God's love," Dad answered.

"We always try to choose a Bible message," Mom added. "See what this one says."

Glory to God in the highest, and on earth peace among men with whom he is pleased (Luke 2:14).

"I know that! It's in our Christmas program," Molly exclaimed. "That's what the angels told the shepherds when they came and said that Jesus was born!"

"Right," Mom answered, smiling. "The dove is one way we make people think of peace, especially at Christmastime."

"We want to share the good news that Jesus, the Prince of Peace, is coming," added Dad.

"Can I send cards to my friends and to my teacher?" Molly asked. "I want to share Christmas peace, too."

PRAY: **Heavenly Father, help me always to share my belief that Christmas brings peace because of Jesus. Amen**

SING: *"It Came upon the Midnight Clear," first stanza (page 38).*

SUGGESTED ACTIVITY: *Each make a list of three to five people with whom you would like to share God's message of peace through Christ. Choose Christmas cards that show something from the Christmas story, or make your own cards.*

READ: One part of the book *Tom Sawyer* tells about Tom being lost in a dark cave with many tunnels and passages. Tom was frightened, but he didn't give up hope until the light from his last candle gave out.

Today after we light the candles, we're going to talk about how light makes us feel.

Light candles. Turn off room lights.

DISCUSS: What do you think of as you see the candlelight flickering in the room? Does the light make you feel peaceful? Or are you afraid with so little light on? Does the candlelight make you feel closer to our family as we sit here together? How does light remind us of Christmas? of Jesus? *(Add any thoughts you might have.)*

Turn on room lights.

READ: When I sit in darkness, the Lord will be a light to me (Micah 7:8).

Let's think of some of the ways lights are used at Christmastime *(candles decorating home and church; lights on trees and houses; family gatherings around fireplaces).*

Why do you think lights are a good way to help people celebrate Jesus' birth? *(A star showed the way to his birthplace; the Bible calls him the "bright morning star"; we are to light the world by following him.)* How can lights be a good way to help people think of peace?

PRAY: Heavenly Father, help me to bring peace to my part of the world. Help me to be a light shining in the darkness. Amen

SING: *"Silent Night," first stanza (page 38).*

Light candles.

READ: Close your eyes and picture in your mind a dark little barn. You can hardly see, but you can smell the hay and hear the animals—cows gently mooing, birds' wings flapping. You notice a tiny light in a far corner, so you carefully feel your way there. The light seems a little brighter, and now you can find your way more easily.

You come to a young woman sitting on some boards; before her in a bed of hay lies a tiny baby. The baby looks at you with big, wise eyes. The light is coming from a small lantern over the manger, but the whole room now seems to glow.

You are at the birthplace of Jesus. It is wonderful to be with him. It is very peaceful here. You wish you never had to leave.

You can open your eyes now.

Some people feel good about the baby Jesus during Christmastime, but seem to forget about him the rest of the year. They forget what a great thing God did in sending his Son to earth. It's too bad if we forget that we can be with Jesus, not just at the manger where we worship our baby King, but in our daily lives as we call on our risen Savior.

Because we know we can be near Jesus in our thoughts, we can have Christmas peace all year round!

Thou dost keep him in perfect peace, whose mind is stayed on thee (Isa. 26.3).

PRAY: Dear God, we praise you for the peace that comes from knowing Jesus. Amen

SING: Away in a manger, no crib for his bed,
The little Lord Jesus laid down his sweet head;
The stars in the sky looked down where he lay,
The little Lord Jesus asleep on the hay.

READ: Let me hear what God the Lord will speak, for he will speak peace to his people (Ps. 85:8).

Shawn came home from confirmation class, set his Bible on the counter, and frowned.

"You look worried," his mother said as she pushed the colored dough through the cookie press.

"It's this passage I read in the Bible," Shawn answered. "We keep saying Jesus is the Prince of Peace, but I found a place where Jesus said he didn't come to bring peace but division. He said people in the same family would be divided —fathers and sons, mothers and daughters. That sounds awful, and not like Jesus at all." *(See Luke 12:51-53.)*

Light candles.

As we light the candles, we wonder how Jesus can really be the Prince of Peace if he said he came to divide families. Yet we **know** that God sent Jesus to bring peace on earth.

There is an enemy who doesn't want people to know they are saved by Jesus. Do you know who it is? The enemy is the devil. He will even use people in our own families to turn us against Jesus, if he can. Families and friends are divided because of Jesus when the devil closes hearts to the truth.

It may seem strange to be talking about the devil right in the middle of our beautiful Christmas preparations, but we need to remember that it is because of the sin and evil the devil brought to God's perfect world in the first place that God needed to send Jesus to die for our sins.

PRAY: Dear God, we pray this Christmas season that everyone in our family will believe in Jesus. That would be the best gift of all. Amen

SING: *"Hark! The Herald Angels Sing," first and second stanzas (page 39).*

Light candles.

READ:

> Dear Heather,
>   I can't believe it's December already! I sure hope you can go to church camp again next summer.
>   We've been using all those pine cones we collected to make wreaths for the neighbors. I just hope we don't have to give one to Mr. Spencer. He's a real grouch.
>   School is pretty good this year, except I have Mrs. Warden. She can't control us kids. I'm glad she's retiring. I joined the art club. We got to paint Christmas scenes in the windows downtown. There's one girl in the club I can't stand—she's so bossy.
>   Christmas shopping has been fun, but I don't know what to get for my dumb brother. I'd like to buy him a one-way ticket to the South Pole.
>   Well, I have to do a current events report for school. I don't like the news. Killings, bombs, wars, nuclear protests — it's all so scary. I wish I could do something to bring peace to the world, but what could little old me do?
>   Merry Christmas!
>
> > > Love,
> > > Janet

Janet needs to do what all peacemakers have learned—to start by making peace right in our own families and communities.

Look at Janet's letter again and decide how she could create peace with the people she named. *(Discuss.)*

Happy are those who work for peace; God will call them his children (Matt. 5:9 TEV).

PRAY: Dear Jesus, let there be peace on earth, and let it begin with me. Amen

SING: *"Silent Night," first and second stanzas (page 38).*

Light candles.

READ: The children helped Dad drag the evergreen from the back of the pickup to the porch. Their snowsuits were wet and their fingers tingled with cold.

"Set your clothes out to dry, and I'll have hot chocolate ready in a jiffy," Mom called, stomping her boots.

Later, as the family sipped steaming cocoa, Kim said, "I hope we can cut our own tree every year. It was fun! We hunted together for just the right one."

"I liked the winter picnic," said Ty.

"I liked the snowball fight," said Johnny.

"It's funny," said Kim, "we were running and being noisy, but it was so peaceful just being together."

Ty added, "I wonder if it will be that kind of peaceful in heaven, or if it's the kind where you sit around on a cloud, playing a harp!"

Mom laughed, "I don't think heaven will be that dull. I think that in heaven we'll have the joyful kind of peace Kim felt today. That kind of peace comes only from God. If we know Jesus we can have peace by a quiet lake or in a noisy crowd."

"Then Jesus really is the Prince of Peace," Johnny said.

Peace I leave with you; my peace I give to you; not as the world gives do I give to you (John 14:27).

PRAY: Dear Jesus, thank you for the peace you brought us when you came to earth. Amen

SING: *"It Came upon the Midnight Clear," first and second stanzas (page 38).*

The Candle of

Joy

As we light the third candle this week, we focus on the theme of joy— the joy we have because we know Jesus is coming and the joy we have because he is with us now.

Sunday   **THIRD WEEK OF ADVENT**

READ: Have you ever been full of joy? Today we'll add a new candle — the **joy candle** — and we'll talk about what joy really means.

Light candles.

"There's nothing to do. I wish I could open my presents now," Jeremy complained.

"Play with the computer football game or the building set you got **last** Christmas,'" Mother suggested.

"I'm tired of those. I want to open my new presents," Jeremy said.

Can you think of a gift you once were really thrilled to get that doesn't seem so exciting now? The presents we get at Christmas may make us happy for a while, but the joy doesn't last forever.

Some joy can last, however, when it's a gift from God. Then we can be joyful whether we're rich or poor, sick or well, shy or popular, and it won't matter so much whether we get ten Christmas presents or one.

We have that joy when we know our sins are forgiven. We have joy, then, in knowing God loves us just the way we are. We have joy in remembering that because Jesus lived on earth awhile we can live with God in heaven forever.

No gift under the tree lasts like that!

Yet I will rejoice in the Lord, I will joy in the God of my salvation (Hab. 3:18).

PRAY: Heavenly Father, the gift of your Son, Jesus, gives me joy at Christmastime and all through the year. Help me to share my joy. Amen

SING: *"Joy to the World," first stanza (page 40).*

You will need a Bible for today's reading.
Light candles.

READ: **When they saw the star, they rejoiced exceedingly with great joy** (Matt. 2:10).

Yesterday we talked about gifts. Do you know who gave the very first Christmas presents? *(the Wise Men in Matthew chapter 2)* What were the gifts? *(gold, frankincense, and myrrh)* Who were the gifts for? *(the baby Jesus)*

Now we're going to hear more about the Wise Men.

Read Matthew 2:1-12.

Notice that the Wise Men weren't **getting** gifts, they were **giving** them, yet they were filled with joy. Why do you like to give gifts? Which is more fun, giving or getting? *(Discuss.)*

PRAY: **Lord, fill me with exceedingly great joy. Help me to give the gift of myself to Jesus. Amen**

SING: We three kings of Orient are:
      Bearing gifts we traverse afar,
      Field and fountain, moor and mountain,
      Following yonder star.
        O star of wonder, star of night,
        Star with royal beauty bright,
        Westward leading, still proceeding,
        Guide us to thy perfect light!

OPTIONAL DISCUSSION *(for older children)*: Why did the Wise Men choose gold, frankincense, and myrrh? How might these gifts have been used?

READ: Yesterday we heard how the Wise Men followed the star, looking for the baby king, Jesus. Herod, the king of the land, got very worried. He was afraid the new king would rise up and take his place. He didn't realize that Jesus wasn't an earthly king.

When the Wise Men didn't return to tell Herod where Jesus was, Herod thought, "If I kill all the baby boys in Bethlehem, I'll be sure to get rid of the new king."

As we light the candles today, let us do so in memory of all the innocent babies who were killed by Herod and his soldiers.

Light candles.

The families of these babies had no joy then. They didn't know their children were the first saints sacrificed for the sake of Jesus. They didn't even know the Savior had been born and that his family had escaped into Egypt.

Someday we might have to suffer because the baby Jesus is our king. But God promises joy to those who suffer for Christ's sake.

But rejoice in so far as you share Christ's sufferings, that you may also rejoice and be glad when his glory is revealed (1 Peter 4:13).

PRAY: Jesus, we pray for all who suffer in your name. Amen

SING: *"Joy to the World," first and third stanzas (page 40).*

READ: Some people share joy during Advent by going Christmas caroling. It's an old custom in which groups of singers go from house to house singing Christmas hymns. They may go to hospitals and homes for elderly people, too.

Light candles.

Carrie had promised she would go caroling with her Sunday school class. But when the day came, she really didn't feel like going. There was a Christmas cartoon special on T.V., and besides, it was cold out! But Carrie went caroling because she had said she would. When only three other children showed up, she thought they should just forget it, but her teacher said they should still go and do the best they could.

Before long, Carrie realized she was having fun. A little baby clapped his hands against the window, and older people smiled like grandparents and even gave them cookies.

Carrie felt a real glow inside when she returned home, and not just from the warm fireplace. It was the glow of joy!

Make a joyful noise to the Lord, all the lands! Serve the Lord with gladness! Come into his presence with singing! (Ps. 100:1-2)

PRAY: Jesus, thank you for the joy that comes from knowing and serving you. Amen

SING: *"Joy to the World,"* first and second stanzas (page 40).

Light candles. Invite the children to say the name of each candle being lit (Family Relationship, Peace, Joy).

SING: *"Hark! The Herald Angels Sing," first and third stanzas (page 39).*

READ: Tanya turned slowly as her mother measured the angel costume.

"Whoever wore this last year was a very tall angel," Mother said, pinning up the hem.

Tanya asked, "Mom, will I be a real angel when I go to heaven?"

"No," Mother answered. "Angels are angels, and people are people. Angels were created by God for different reasons than were people."

"An angel told Mary she was going to have a baby," said Tanya. "And angels told the shepherds the Savior was born. Is that what they're for? To tell things?"

Mother answered, "Yes, they're messengers. But they help God in many ways. It was angels who shut the lions' mouths when Daniel was in the lions' den. The Bible says God gives his angels charge over us to help keep us safe."

"I still think their best job was announcing that Jesus was born," Tanya said.

"Well, that's something we can do too, just like the angels," Mother said. "We can tell everyone the good news of great joy, that to us is born a Savior, who is Christ the Lord."

Just so, I tell you, there is joy before the angels of God over one sinner who repents (Luke 15:10).

PRAY: Lord, help me to be as joyous as the angels in telling the good news about Jesus. Amen

READ: Are you like Brian? Brian kept hearing that Jesus will come back again some day, but he didn't know if he really believed it. Every day just came and went the same as always. He really couldn't imagine Jesus interrupting the whole thing.

Light candles.

Remember what Advent means? It means Jesus is coming.

Think of the people who lived before Jesus was born. For hundreds of years God had promised them a Savior. The people kept watching and waiting, but it seemed the promised Savior would never come. Then suddenly it was the first Christmas! There Jesus was!

At times it may seem to us that Jesus has forgotten to come back. Yet we can be sure he will return. God will keep this promise just as he kept the promise of sending a Savior to the people hundreds of years ago. What joy there will be then!

The Lord reigns; let the earth rejoice (Ps. 97:1).

SING: *"Oh, Come, Oh, Come, Emmanuel," first stanza (page 40).*

PRAY: Come, Lord Jesus. Amen

Light candles.

READ: The call came just as Marion's family was leaving for the church Christmas concert. Grandma Hanson had died.

The family sat down in the living room and waited for Uncle Herb and Aunt Esther to come plan for the funeral. Everyone cried.

"How can we have a joyful Christmas with Grandma gone?" asked Marion. "This will be the saddest Christmas ever."

"And we'll think about it every year at Christmas," Tim added, nervously fiddling with a toy sheep from the manger scene.

"We'll be sad because there will be an empty spot in our hearts for Grandma," Dad answered. "But we have to remember what Christmas is. It's God coming to earth to show us that death is not the end.

"The disciples felt like you do now when Jesus was crucified. They didn't think they'd ever have joy again. But Jesus kept his promise of life and returned from the grave at Easter. And that's the promise of Christmas.

"We have two reasons to be joyful this Christmas. One is that Jesus is coming. The other is that Grandma, too, lives because Jesus died and rose again."

For this day is holy to our Lord; and do not be grieved, for the joy of the Lord is your strength (Neh. 8:10).

PRAY: Dear God, sad things happen, even at Christmas. Let your joy keep us strong. Amen

SING: *"Joy to the World," first, second, and third stanzas (page 40).*

The Candle of

Love

God, who is love, acted out this attribute in history by sending his only Son to suffer for our sins. During this final week of Advent we will light the candle of love to remind us just how great and costly God's love is.

Sunday   **FOURTH WEEK OF ADVENT**

READ: Our new candle today is called the **love candle**.

Light candles.

During this last week in Advent we will think a lot about love as we gather around our wreath. Most often we show love not just by what we **say** to others, but by what we **do** for them.

A certain woman was very ill and knew it would be her last Christmas. All her life she had wanted a record player, but she had never had enough money to buy one.

This woman's son had a good-paying job. He loved his mother very much, so he gave her a record player for Christmas. The gift gave her much pleasure before she died, but the love her son had shown her gave her even more joy.

God did something like that once for a man called Simeon. God had promised Simeon he would not die until he had seen the Savior. Now Simeon was very old, and he still had not seen the promised one. One day when he was at the temple, some parents brought their baby. The parents were Joseph and Mary, and the baby was Jesus. The Holy Spirit told Simeon this baby was the Savior. The Bible tells us how Simeon felt:

Now, Lord, you have kept your promise, and you may let your servant go in peace. With my own eyes I have seen your salvation, which you have prepared in the presence of all peoples: A light to reveal your will to the Gentiles and bring glory to your people Israel (Luke 2:29-32 TEV).

Simeon was rejoicing because God loved him enough to keep his promise and because God loved the world enough to send a Savior.

PRAY: Heavenly Father, thank you for showing us your wonderful love. Amen

SING: *"Oh, Come, All Ye Faithful," first stanza (page 40).*

31

READ: What is the name of our new candle? *(Love candle)*

Light candles.

If I speak in the tongues of men and of angels, but have not love, I am a noisy gong or a clanging cymbal (1 Cor. 13:1).

Bells jangling from Christmas booths on busy streets remind us to give to the poor. Silver bells decorating windows are a beautiful sight. Bells ringing in a steeple call us to Christmas worship. Bells are a symbol of Christmas!

Ancient Romans who were not Christians used bells to announce that big pools, called "baths," were open. Later, the Christians in Rome took over the ringing of bells to announce worship services.

Soon great church towers with large bells were built near and far. The bells woke people in the morning and reminded them to pray. The bells rang four times every hour all day long. They also rang at special times like weddings, funerals, Easter, and Christmas.

Today bells are a fine symbol for Christmas because they ring out the joyful news that our Savior is born. We too can be like bells, singing out the birth of Christ, sharing God's love. But if we make anything other than Jesus the most important part of our Christmas (like presents, parties, food), then we aren't Christmas bells. Instead we're just noisy gongs.

PRAY: Lord, help me to be a bell of love, proclaiming Christ's birth to everyone. Amen

SING: *"Joy to the World," first stanza (page 40).*

SUGGESTED ACTIVITY: *Make a Christmas bell decoration. Poke yarn or string, with knotted ends up, through inverted paper cups. (Use cups with a Christmas design, or cover others with foil.) Tie pieces of yarn in a bow at the top.*

Light candles.

READ: Love bears all things, believes all things, hopes all things, endures all things (1 Cor. 13:7).

Let's listen to an ancient Christmas legend about a robin.

It was a very cold night. Joseph, Mary, and the baby Jesus had fallen asleep in the stable. They didn't know their fire was going out. Soon only a few coals were flickering.

In flew a little robin, sent by God. He perched by the dying fire and began fanning the coals with his wings. As the wood began to spark again and then burn, the robin's breast turned red from the heat. Still the determined bird would not quit. He continued to flap his wings until there was a roaring fire which would not go out again.

Ever since then robins have had a red breast, a symbol of love and devotion for the baby Jesus.

Of course, this is not a true story. It's only a legend, told and retold over the years to remind us that Jesus is so wonderful we should be willing to do anything for him. We should love Jesus **that** much!

PRAY: Dear Jesus, we could never do enough to repay your love. Still, help us to love you as you have loved us. Amen

SING: *"Oh, Come, All Ye Faithful," first and second stanzas (page 40).*

READ: Imagine a God who loves us so much that he came to live with us.

Light candles.

. . . **and his name shall be called Emmanuel (which means, God with us)** (Matt. 1:23).

There is a story about a man who had a big window in his living room. Birds couldn't tell that the clear opening was really glass, and they kept flying into it. The man went outside and tried to teach the birds not to fly there, but he only frightened them. Finally the man thought, "Oh, if only I could make myself a bird like them for a while. Then I could go among them and show them how to be safe from danger. The birds would know I really cared about them and meant them no harm."

God once looked down on his created people and saw they were having trouble. They were falling deeper and deeper in sin. They didn't know how much God loved them. They did not know that he would forgive them if they would trust in him and turn from their sins. Many people were afraid of God. God thought, "Oh, if I could just become one of those people for a while, I would go among them and show them the way out of sin. I could show them how much I care."

Of course, the man in our story couldn't become a bird. But God, being God almighty, could become a human. And he did! He came to earth as the baby Jesus to show us the way out of our sin. He came to show us that we can be forgiven. He came so we would not fear him but would understand his love.

PRAY: Dear Lord, you came to live with us as God the Son. Thank you for being Emmanuel. Amen

SING: *"Hark! The Herald Angels Sing," second stanza (page 39).*

READ: Today as we light the candles of family relationship, peace, joy, and love, we think of the special love Jesus showed for children. *(Light candles.)*

"Christmas is for children." Have you heard that before?

Grown-ups often say that Christmas is for children because Christmas brings back special memories of their own childhoods: Grandma and Grandpa's nativity set on the mantel; Mother's homemade fudge; the family stringing popcorn for the tree; Father carving the turkey for dinner.

Then as grown-ups, they see the familiar sparkle in their own children's eyes as they hear the Christmas story or place a special angel atop the tree or unwrap a Christmas secret hidden in brightly colored paper.

Christmas is for children, because it was Jesus himself who gathered children in his arms and showed them his love. And to think that the disciples wanted to send the little ones away so they wouldn't "bother" Jesus!

But Christmas is for grown-ups, too. Jesus came for everyone: young or old; poor or rich; red, black, yellow, brown, or white.

Try never to lose the excitement you now feel over the arrival of the baby Jesus. Treasure the miracle of his birth whether you are teenaged, middle-aged, or elderly. Celebrating Christmas with the wonder of a child will help your love for Jesus to grow and grow.

And calling to him a child, he . . . said, "Truly, I say to you, unless you turn and become like children, you will never enter the kingdom of heaven (Matt. 18:2-3).

PRAY: Dear Jesus, you never forgot what it was like to be a little child. Help me never to forget either. Amen

SING: *"Oh, Come, All Ye Faithful," first stanza (page 40).*

READ: Little children, let us not love in word or speech but in deed and in truth (1 John 3:18). *(Light candles.)*

Eric was unhappy. It was Christmas Day, and he had to go with his family to the rescue mission to help serve Christmas dinner to people who had no food or money. He knew that was a good thing to do, but he wanted to stay home and play with his new toys. "I'll bet I'll be the only kid there. I wouldn't even have to go if my dad wasn't a pastor."

Imagine Eric's surprise when he saw kids his own age setting the tables: Amber and Elizabeth, Mike and George.

"What are **you** doing here?" Eric asked Amber. "Your dad's not a pastor."

"Oh, this is our third year to help here," exclaimed Amber. "It's fun! See that old man? He gave me this locket last year because he doesn't have any grandchildren. So this year I gave him a book of Bible verses I got at Sunday school."

"One of the cooks says I remind her of her son when he was little," added Mike, "so she saves me an extra piece of pie!"

"You mean you **like** giving up your Christmas to come here and help?" asked Eric.

"Give up?" laughed Elizabeth. "How can we be 'giving up' our Christmas when we're coming here to share our love and when we get so much in return?"

"Come on, Eric. Help me with the chairs. It won't take you long to see what we mean," George said, tugging at Eric's sleeve.

Eric caught a big whiff of roast turkey coming from the kitchen. "I'm beginning to see already," he said as he followed George down an aisle of chairs.

PRAY: Dear God, help me not just to say I love people. Let me also show it by my actions. Amen

SING: *"Joy to the World,"* first and third stanzas *(page 40).*

Light candles. Say the name of each candle being lit (Family Relationship, Peace, Joy, Love).

READ: For God so loved the world that he gave his only Son, that whoever believes in him should not perish but have eternal life (John 3:16).

If we had to give a meaning for Christmas in one word, love would be the best word we could choose.

Let us read the beautiful Christmas story from the Bible. As we hear it, let's remember that God planned, produced, and directed this magnificent happening out of a special love for each one of us.

Read Luke 2:1-20.

Repeat today's Bible verse for each person present, inserting his or her name:

For God so loved _____ name _____ that he gave his only Son, that _____ name _____, believing in him, should not perish but have eternal life.

PRAY: Glory to God in the highest, and on earth peace, goodwill to all. Amen

SING: *"Silent Night," first and second stanzas (page 38).*

Hymns

You may choose to sing a favorite hymn not printed here.

1 **Children of the heav'nly Father**
  Safely in his bosom gather;
  Nestling bird or star in heaven
  Such a refuge ne'er was given.

2 God his own doth tend and nourish,
  In his holy courts they flourish.
  From all evil things he spares them,
  In his mighty arms he bears them.

3 Neither life nor death shall ever
  From the Lord his children sever;
  Unto them his grace he showeth,
  And their sorrows all he knoweth.

1 **Silent night, holy night!**
  All is calm, all is bright
  Round yon virgin mother and child.
  Holy Infant, so tender and mild,
  Sleep in heavenly peace,
  Sleep in heavenly peace.

2 Silent night, holy night!
  Shepherds quake at the sight;
  Glories stream from heaven afar,
  Heav'nly hosts sing, Alleluia!
  Christ, the Savior, is born!
  Christ, the Savior, is born!

1 **It came upon the midnight clear,**
  That glorious song of old,
  From angels bending near the earth
  To touch their harps of gold:
  "Peace on the earth, good will to all,
  From heav'n's all-gracious king."
  The world in solemn stillness lay
  To hear the angels sing.

2 Still through the cloven skies they come
   With peaceful wings unfurled,
   And still their heav'nly music floats
   O'er all the weary world.
   Above its sad and lowly plains
   They bend on hov'ring wing,
   And ever o'er its babel sounds
   The blessed angels sing.

1 **Hark! The herald angels sing,**
   "Glory to the newborn king;
   Peace on earth, and mercy mild,
   God and sinners reconciled."
   Joyful, all you nations, rise;
   Join the triumph of the skies;
   With angelic hosts proclaim,
   "Christ is born in Bethlehem!"
       Hark! The herald angels sing,
       "Glory to the newborn king!"

2 Christ, by highest heav'n adored,
   Christ, the everlasting Lord,
   Late in time behold him come,
   Offspring of a virgin's womb.
   Veiled in flesh the Godhead see!
   Hail, incarnate deity!
   Pleased as man with us to dwell,
   Jesus, our Emmanuel!
       Hark! The herald angels sing,
       "Glory to the newborn king!"

3 Hail the heav'n-born Prince of Peace!
   Hail the sun of righteousness!
   Light and life to all he brings,
   Ris'n with healing in his wings.
   Mild he lays his glory by,
   Born that we no more may die,
   Born to raise each child of earth,
   Born to give us second birth.
       Hark! The herald angels sing,
       "Glory to the newborn king!"

1 **Joy to the world, the Lord is come!**
Let earth receive its King;
Let ev'ry heart prepare him room
And heav'n and nature sing,
And heav'n and nature sing,
And heav'n, and heav'n and nature sing.

2 Joy to the earth, the Savior reigns!
Let all their songs employ,
While fields and floods, rocks, hills, and plains
Repeat the sounding joy,
Repeat the sounding joy,
Repeat, repeat the sounding joy.

3 He rules the world with truth and grace
And makes the nations prove
The glories of his righteousness
And wonders of his love,
And wonders of his love,
And wonders, wonders of his love.

1 **Oh, come, oh, come, Emmanuel,**
And ransom captive Israel,
That mourns in lonely exile here
Until the Son of God appear.
Rejoice! Rejoice! Emmanuel
Shall come to you, O Israel.

1 **Oh, come, all ye faithful,** joyful and triumphant!
Oh, come ye, oh, come ye to Bethlehem;
Come and behold him born the king of angels;
Oh, come, let us adore him,
Oh, come, let us adore him,
Oh, come, let us adore him, Christ the Lord!

2 Sing choirs of angels, sing in exultation,
Sing, all ye citizens of heaven above!
Glory to God in the highest:
Oh, come, let us adore him,
Oh, come, let us adore him,
Oh, come, let us adore him, Christ the Lord!